Billie Jean King

A Little Golden Book® Biography

By Anna Membrino • Illustrated by Jen Bricking

A GOLDEN BOOK • NEW YORK

Golden Books
An imprint of Random House Children's Books
A division of Penguin Random House LLC
1745 Broadway, New York, NY 10019
penguinrandomhouse.com
rhcbooks.com

Library of Congress Control Number: 2024953053
ISBN 979-8-217-02547-3 (trade) — ISBN 979-8-217-02548-0 (ebook)
Manufactured in the United States of America
10 9 8 7 6 5 4 3 2 1
EU Contact: Penguin Random House Ireland, 32 Nassau Street, Dublin D02 YH68.
https://eu-contact.penguin.ie

Billie Jean King was born Billie Jean Moffitt on November 22, 1943, in Long Beach, California. She grew up to be one of the best tennis players in the world and a famous activist.

Billie Jean had two things growing up: a strong sense of right and wrong and a love for sports.

As a young girl, Billie Jean ran races, rode bikes, and played baseball and touch football with the neighborhood kids. She was a natural athlete.

Sometimes the boys tried to leave Billie Jean out. Her dad told them they weren't allowed on his lawn unless his daughter could play, too. That changed their minds pretty quickly.

Billie Jean didn't like feeling excluded. When it was time to pick teams for games, she made sure that everyone got to play and that the least athletic kids weren't picked last.

If she or her younger brother Randy saw someone getting picked on at school, they became the "anti-bullying squad." The other kids noticed and started electing Billie Jean as a leader. They made her captain of the glee club, even though she was the worst singer in the group!

Billie Jean and her dad loved playing basketball together, taking shots at the hoop hanging above their garage. She was also the shortstop on a softball team. But her world changed when she was eleven years old and her friend Susan invited her to play tennis.

Billie Jean said, “What’s tennis?”

Susan explained that you could run, jump, and hit a ball. All of that sounded fun to Billie Jean!

Billie Jean was terrible at tennis at first. She even whacked a ball over the fence and shouted, "Home run!" Susan thought that was funny. The other people at the tennis club did *not* think it was funny.

She wasn't good, but she was hooked. Tennis was hard, and Billie Jean loved the challenge. After her first day of real lessons, she told her mom that she wanted to be the number one tennis player in the world. Her mom said, "Okay, dear."

When Billie Jean wasn't taking lessons, she was practicing tennis at home. She spent every spare moment hitting balls against a wooden fence at her house. Her dad put up a spotlight so she could keep hitting at night.

She lost her first tournament match in the junior division to her friend Susan. But that just made her want to win more! She kept practicing and improving. When she was only fifteen, Billie Jean was good enough to move from the junior division to the women's division!

She was playing so well that a man with a lot of money who loved tennis wanted to pay to send her to England to compete at Wimbledon, the oldest and most famous tennis tournament in the world. She appreciated the offer but told him she wasn't ready yet.

She worked really hard, and just two years later, she was ranked fourth in the United States in singles and doubles. When that same man asked again if she wanted to go to Wimbledon, Billie Jean said yes!

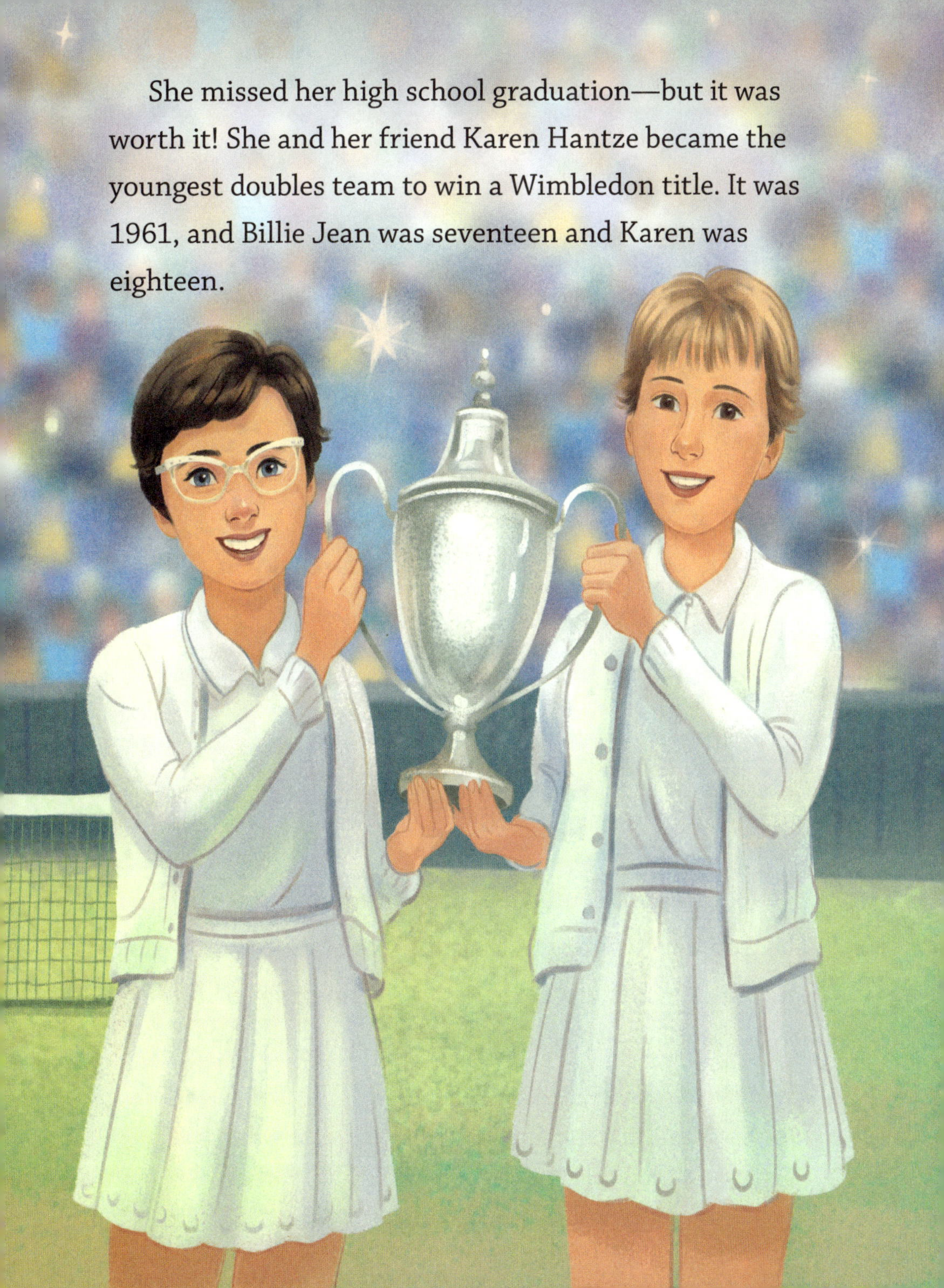

She missed her high school graduation—but it was worth it! She and her friend Karen Hantze became the youngest doubles team to win a Wimbledon title. It was 1961, and Billie Jean was seventeen and Karen was eighteen.

Billie Jean was on the rise as a tennis star. In 1966, she won her first Grand Slam singles title at Wimbledon and was the number one women's tennis player in the world. But she still couldn't earn a living playing tennis. No woman could. When they won tournaments, they were paid half, sometimes even a third, of what the men were paid.

Famous tennis champion Althea Gibson had quit the sport in 1958. She explained, "You can't eat trophies."

It was time for things to change.

Change was happening all around the country. The civil rights movement was growing quickly, and people were demanding equal rights for all.

Billie Jean was also demanding justice. On the court, she was getting a reputation as a chatterbox. She spoke up when she thought something was unfair. She was a chatterbox off the court, too. She argued for equal opportunities for women and men and for equal prize money in tennis.

She told a reporter that women's sports stories needed to be featured in the newspaper just like the articles on men's sports. She complained that tennis was mostly accessible to rich white kids. Why couldn't everyone play the sport she loved?

Billie Jean kept pushing for change. Now that she was the number one player in the world, people listened. The president of the USLTA (United States Lawn Tennis Association) told her he would suspend her if she didn't keep quiet. But she kept talking.

Billie Jean accomplished big things in 1973. Not only did she win singles, doubles, and mixed doubles at Wimbledon that year, but she founded and became the president of the Women's Tennis Association. In a huge victory, she also convinced the USLTA to award equal prize money to women and men at that year's US Open.

Billie Jean was fighting for change and making it happen!

The tennis player Bobby Riggs didn't like the things she was saying. He didn't think women deserved to be paid the same as men. Not even close! He challenged Billie Jean to a match to prove once and for all that men were better than women.

Billie Jean thought Bobby was a bully. But she knew that the match could make a difference. She wanted girls to be able to have the same dreams as any boy. So she agreed to play him.

On September 20, 1973, ninety million people worldwide tuned in to watch what the media called The Battle of the Sexes. Bobby Riggs was confident, but he was no match for Billie Jean. She had studied his game and worked hard.

She beat him fair and square, in three straight sets!

Since that match, things slowly started to improve for women athletes and women's sports. While the US Open offered men and women equal prize money in 1973, it took decades for the other Grand Slam tournaments to do the same.

Every year, more and more girls are playing sports. The number of viewers watching women's soccer, tennis, and basketball keeps growing.

Billie Jean King helped pave the way!

In 2009, Billie Jean was awarded the Presidential Medal of Freedom by President Obama. He honored what Billie Jean calls "all the off-the-court stuff" that she has done for women's rights and to help make the future brighter for everyone in the LGBTQ+ community.

Billie Jean continues to support women in sports. She advises the Professional Women's Hockey League. And she and her wife, Ilana Kloss, are part owners of the National Women's Soccer League team Angel City FC.

Billie Jean's love of sports and strong sense of right and wrong still guide everything she does. She wants to make the world a better place—and she does just that!